5 3

9

9 5 3 9

9 0

7 8

4 *1*

6 2

8

7

1

4

2

6

0

Persuasion for a Mathematician | Joanne Page

PEDLAR
PRESS

PEDLAR PRESS
PO Box 26, Station P, Toronto Ontario M5S 2S6 Canada

ACKNOWLEDGEMENTS. The publisher gratefully acknowledges the financial support of the Canada Council for the Arts and the Ontario Arts Council for its publishing program.

Edited for the press by Erin Mouré.

NATIONAL LIBRARY OF CANADA CATALOGUING IN PUBLICATION

Page, Joanne
        Persuasion for a mathematician / Joanne Page.
        — 1st ed.
Poems.
ISBN 0-9732140-3-1
        I. Title.
PS8581.A383P47 2003   C811'.54   C2003-902650-7
PR9199.3.P275P47 2003

First Edition

DESIGN Zab Design & Typography
COVER ART Ryan Price
Printed in Canada

Persuasion for a Mathematician

Contents

Kite

Lie down in unfenced prairie,
look at the sky.
It is all there, everything,
first daylight, last,
and when you look back
its blue will be the most raw, fullest,
nothing like a dream.

At that time, you will say,
The world was an artful mercy,
And people original and precious
for their lost-and-foundness,
rinsing gold from the stream a daily business
on city streets you thought you knew
well enough,

summer nights, their darkness an annihilation
of a kind you never understood before, deeper;
the audible slow burn of stars left you rapt, you will say,
sepals and petals and visions of retreat were hung engravings
on days pitched and gullied, grasslands running up to ravine,
and below, its silver keel rivers on,
instrument of restlessness
that will bear you through.

I

A Dark Wood

Nel mezzo del cammin di nostra vita
mi ritrovai per una selva oscura,
che la diritta via era smarrita.

Midway in the journey of our life
I found myself in a dark wood
for the straight way was lost.

— DANTE ALIGHIERI, COMMEDIA

Half a Correspondence

May 3

Dear Jan,

What I saw when I met you:

anticipation: a person positioned so as to be ready for
a lifetime; more: buttery yellow dress I later learned you chose
so you would look a daffodil in April, official flower, settled
in a room among welcoming women, and when I asked
how you were doing you made mention of

these travails that flesh falls heir to and I felt compelled
to ponder your cranium, that storage bin, painted in crayon colours
like the bed linen you showed us, stuffed with arcane
expressions, legal preamble, stray formulae from the periodic
table, blackthorn cudgels, items, as your mother would say,
to keep "at heart" as these next months unfold and you sort
what is necessary

into what time remains.

This letter is only to say that I know too well the landscape
of terror where you find yourself, and pursuant to that

want to be delivered into your corner
with supplies for the haul
to the height above the sun
where the firmament reserves its absent light.

July 21

Dear Jan,

Breathing space and
questionable procedures:
two days in a row I have sought a fugitive in green
going downstream a little faster than the rest of us.
I find you under the scanner, hanging onto a guarantee
not issued.

You grab your smile,
tiny offering in this radiantland,
Nuclear Medicine being out of licorice allsorts.
No, the only trade here is in bones, my dear,
restless bones, ivory castanets,
scaffolding of the heart.

Sidelined temporarily in the catacomb,
subdued to someone you are not,
I looked Death in the face, you say, *and He
blinked.*

Here is the exact moment for wild tulip meadows,
             for higher songbirds,
                          orioles in the arboreal forest crown,

     cinnamon, slide guitars
                          a three-day Legion dance,
                 an absence of liars.

Who would it help you to know
in these days longer than their length,

itinerant Aladdin in resplendent silk, a festival of clowns,
or the pastry chef from Rideau Hall, why stint, who's counting
costs, can it be so hard, can you laugh again, may I take your
hand, can I will you out of here?

Dear Jan,

Much to do with dying is skid,
unforeseen douse of lake water on hot rock.

In truth neither sorcery nor already-written scripture
will turn this autumn holy:

there is only the laying on of solid colour,
sky thrown down behind trees, torrential and finally

blue, the divide between high ground and the galaxy,
your red hair exclamation mark.

These burning white days, their fluted edges,
when much to do with love is waiting

to be held, without judgement,
including the parts you would disallow

if you could, your friends, me,
at you to let us closer,

running out of time, and your body
a chorus of cells belting out a song against extinction.

September 25

Dear Jan,

Today
the first treatment,

you looked not bad
which is to say that you opened the door,
served me canned soup, Campbell's Golden Mushroom,

flung out the quilt, peopled further, new add-ons,
and we laughed about who is permanent
who is merely glued on
and therefore removable
at whim,
neither of us saying the obvious:
that not one of us is here to stay,
and you walk as though
even the air through which you move injures,

knowing, you said, that a whole lot
doesn't make any difference,
that what will eventuate
is pretty much what's going to happen, meaning:
another woman alone
at the unexpected intersection
of what is necessary
with how to take a run at additional time
and greater comfort and being sure of your kids,
sorting through medical choices
for peace of mind.

All the carrot juice in the world, you say,
won't do much more than a couple of glasses
of tap water, won't interrupt what is already in motion.

Wind
blowing restlessly

downs the first leaves,
we get out our appointment books,
undertake a prolonged discussion about food,
menus, leading to a plan
and we get right down to it,
a date finally agreed on
with much describing and re-describing of location,
this affordable yet delicious restaurant,
to prolong the pleasure of having been smart enough
to pin down an occasion when five of us —
damsels, we call ourselves —
can get together: important
to peg in an ordinary minor pleasure:
critical.

Quieter, each morning a fistful of motionless trees,
costumed, regal,
pillars holding apart the air and the earth
for one more day.

I would wrap it, deliver it to you
in the western suburbs of this
greystone city full of penitents
ticking days off their calendars toward release.
Some freedoms look like cinders, some like gold
in a moving stream:
limit, source, the whole glittering dance.

October 10

Dear Jan

Who is this woman who seized the crowd by its unsuspecting neck?
Shop around, she said, check out the sales on burial at sea and cenotaphs;
each day, she said, a sheaf of naked foolscap. Who is this woman on the
stage of the university hall wearing hair a shade too red, and sculpted to
within an inch of its life? Her listeners never guessing the one choice
permitted: that the story is about a figure at the edge of a landscape, a
comic harlequin under the aegis of a unicorn, playing random songs on a
keyboard, inaccessible as the biographical details of a feather.

Dear Jan

Barb's birthday:
You under your wig
in the corner chair
chosen for strategic purpose
in case you had to suddenly make a break
for it, having quilted your brains out all week
so as to have the gift
in a tolerable state of readiness,
changing your mind about the colours
at the twelfth hour
and making another
(you intended one for each of us),
everyone commenting on the length
and distance between the stitches,
a hit, a sensation, a downright wonder
considering how under the weather
you were as late as Tuesday evening.
I have to think that if you were tied up
and lowered to the depths of a forty-foot well
and left to your own devices for two days
you'd have three or twenty quilts
neatly piled on your forehead
when we reeled you back
into this company of fierce companions.

Other gifts:
bag of popcorn
glass bowl broadly curved
journal
wooden basket with apple
mobile of seed-bearing plants
red clay mask
handmade table linens
work of recent fiction
merriment and
bold stories of engineering gadgets
found in builders' supply depots
on a Friday night crawl.

This celebration loosens
scent over tawny barrenlands,
a quiet plume of air that
returns the future to a distance
between mountains,
a rift valley
of ungovernable flowers.

Dear Jan,

Today puts you halfway.

Time left with you in it is a picture,
the picture with you in it has left time,
abandoned calendar and clock,
become a drumming chamber,
your country music heart
that got toughened up by being
wrecked a couple of times,
stomped on.

Very heart
which will injure a crowd of others
including mine when its beat hesitates,
stops. Where is the sense in the mathematics
taking you and leaving Clifford Olsen?
How to understand a late and lasting flourish
of polished leaves shot through with sun
as your chemicals spill, get torched, flare?

Dear Jan,

Breakthrough:
yesterday in the blue of November's sweetest ache,
downtown for treatment,
me preceding,
determined you won't slip by
and get buried in the warren
of rooms,
unfindable;
you turn up breathless,
your smile a bulletproof vest,
I stick to you like porridge.

Consultation:
in a room
cold enough to flash-freeze,
jokes about forgetting to
pay the heating bill,
out flat on the bed
under a thermal blanket
and several flannel sheets,
you breathing too fast,
too shallow
to rosy up your cheeks;
we shift
oncologist and nurse
undo, unlayer,

tapping down the spine
listening for a crackle,
your back unprotected
and I want to wrap you up with my arms
make you into a temperate zone.

Treatment:
another glacier dispensing poison,
tiny drops inside plastic vacuum packs,
fluid into a major vessel —
scarlet in your case —
wild poppy red, spectral.

Ordeal:
white tray,
surgical gloves,
does this hurt, hon?
iodine wiped on,
and off,
the square cotton patch,
fingers kneading,
sorry, sorry,
needing the outline,
thought we were in,
pinned down,
slender steel,
maybe sitting up
would be better,

into your skin,
hand to hand, stronghold;
*I don't want to hurt you
sweetie,*
five times,
finally!
crimson blessing
fast up the needle
Yes!

What fell away:
in that moment like vapour against sun,
how you've held yourself apart all these years,
not wanting to put anyone out, what you learned,
your mother who does it well,
so many decades of practice, no limit to the means.

The end:
protection against freefall, against the hurtling cliff-leap into the ether,
what we do if we trust.

It's that easy:
we will not speak of disappointment or foregone events,
we will not tell stories we cannot believe,
we will not permit useless options,
we will not travel down detours or upstream,
we will not learn anything but a glad song,
we will not go back;
we will receive fruit at the door
and sing the lowering sun
beyond snow ridges and breakers into spring.

November 13

Dear Jan

this is the night, hard breathing, pain increasing,

breathing, breathing, the oxygen on, off, pause, on, off, pause, cat pacing back and forth between us, visiting nurse beside you on the couch taking vital signs. a worry: pulse up, pressure down, temperature low enough to hardly make vertical, although you maintain you are hot. you were always hot, my dear.

she phones to find out how worried we ought to be. no problem, says covering oncologist, if she wants to be at home, that's where she should stay (or words to that effect), thereby confirming one final time that you are in charge and what you want is, will be, must be, what will happen.

a fast trip for me to the pharmacy for morphine at closing time, rapid tear-streaked trip and long wait in the near-empty store, back again to hickorywood, driving carefully, a night for precision.

you under the red and yellow quilt, waiting, nurse gone, and we get one of the pills into you, pronto. pull up the drawbridge, you say, and I grapple with the uncooperative locking mechanism at the front door, leave the keys on the kitchen counter. we settle in for *scarlet*, *episode one*, between puffing breaths, your struggle for oxygen filling the space between us, occupying the room, is the only sound in the universe, might extinguish the stars.

eleven-thirty: another couple of ginger ales, one each. I'm on the other couch under the apricot quilt from upstairs, you are upright, can't lie back on the pillows. I wonder how you are going to sleep sitting up. the answer is that you aren't; breathing is a full-time job.

one o'clock: listening, breathe in, breathe out, the rhythm of the pump, cat from your couch to mine to the window, an equilateral triangle in starlight.

two-thirty: more ginger ale, ice, you are slumped forward over the two small pillows, no quilt.

three o'clock: sick, mop-up, towels, I'm dizzy, sweating, upstairs and get sick too, might as well be in this together, both of us on your couch now, I hold you.

three-thirty: sick again, I have defiled the couch, you say, in your little-girl voice, you smile, I smile, you are feeling really bad? I ask, you nod. we've got options, I say, we can call the nurse again and get more drugs. you think about that for a while, we sit still.

three-forty: I think, you say slowly, that we can't do this much longer. I want this to be your call. we look at each other, your breath faster, the machine pumps on, you say:

I think we have to go.

Elegy

no bringing you back
no losing you,

the tire tracks scored deep
your front lawn held the lines for seven days,

the stretcher
going downtown,
right hand turns all the way,
one last try at standup,
discard the wig and costumes, the half-finished quilt
thread-drawn daisies
tacked close-hauled across sea green cotton
voyaging over your dining room table.

last gift:
the iv-drip,
my arms our words now,
your hands flutter
irregular signals.
just get to sunrise, I promise you,
and the worst will be over

breathing together,
you, me, the machine
labouring,
our lungs rowers sweeping through to the final reach,

your life a silvered wake turning over,
overturning, behind us,

you bent over your knees

this restlessness

here it comes

I think I'm going

the punishing neon hospital light,
your eyes.

November 23

Dear Jan,

I gotta tell you it's late November,
    the weather remains mostly clear —
    keep the bright skies coming, sweetheart,
    we'll get to Christmas baking later in the month
    or whenever we stop expecting your next entrance.

You ought to know:
    those roses of yours kept blooming
    in the Gardens of Babylon among the fountains
    and tea rooms, the terraced levels stepped
    down to the deer park known as Cataraqui Woods,

    where anyone else might have considered
    a couple of russet chrysanthemums for late fall
    you planted briar rose,
    it held a good two weeks,
    all that oxygen, maybe,
    seeping out, adhering.

Get busy,
    with the single random acts,
    contracts, proposed subversion,
    chains of unexplained events
    to unhitch that ex of yours
    from surplus money or his wife:
    churls and cretins flung in disarray.

One thing though,
      I need your number.
      The matter is I miss our evening calls,
      your voice breathless
      distilled to a higher note,
      making me think I've interrupted
      a chemistry experiment
      or the re-enactment of a principle
      of physics, maybe centrifugal force:
      your kitchen spinning,
      coconut shreds pasted to the walls,
      macadamia nuts,
      earrings and chicken feet slippers,
      quilts sailing over the western township,
      wealth of soft cotton tucking the stars in
      their fleet light extinguished
            the long day journey begun.

Summer Ice

for Bronwen Wallace

Row of Poplars

The summer after the great ice storm
I come to the lake to watch the row of amputated trees
awning their heights with green

and hear wind insinuate itself in the canopy
chinking leaves like coinage, currency of another
August's garden, poplars, plunder —

and the preoccupation of nine
years turns over
and sinks under its accumulation.

What did it matter who was there?
No one could have saved her.

Trance

Summer heat returns me:
the long hours of afternoon when pain held the whip hand,
she down to her bones lying in air drawn from lawns
through the bedroom window, colour dissolving in a watery gleam
which spared nothing, her eyes black pearls, her mouth dust dry.

Do you want to see it? and I behind her at the bathroom sink
helpless to refuse. She untapes the two sides, her cheek bared,
our eyes in the mirror, locked. If she can meet this death,
I can hold her eyes from its vicious brand for as long as I have to.

Arrangement of Notes

Among ticks and hourly chimes the clock hides time,
on the street a work crew, hammer and tongs,
bombardment percusses concrete to rubble, doing away
with contemplation (any hope of making sense),
the flayed silence every bit as prophetic
as leaves arrayed in an overturned tea cup.
From his cage in the garden the cockatiel sounds his bell
four times — Do Not For Get — devoid of news the phone calls out
intermittently to the fridge the washer the blender the dryer.
Upstairs a vivisector inaudible, juggernaut composer of this score,
takes her flesh like a flensing knife, and she tap-tapping lightly
fingers the gauze over the hot black hole.

The white bird screams and oh, the almighty shambles of it twists and
stretches to vibrato, the cicada, on and on and on —

The Healing Circle

To be amusing she wrote it would be like a grade school party
meaning *not all of you will be picked*
and we the waiting hoped to be and hoped not,
we the waiting, the tenders, the helpers, the helpless,
wanting to know and wanting not to,
waiting it out.

Word came down the date was set,
the names selected, parts composed,
and we the chosen searched for words that were not lies.

If I could go again into that room, if I could
slowly make my way to her street through the right-of-way
across the baseball diamond, if I were to spend
a day culling lies from what is honest,
from me there would be no talk of healing, of fixing or mending,
for I knew it to be useless and did not say.

When she told me *put your hand on my head
and think water*, I would place my hand and think water.
When it came my turn to speak I would say only *love*.

Watermelon Smoothies

The more food the garden grew the less she ate
until it was down to watermelon mostly,
seeded, yellow-green rind cut away,
chunks of pink clean taste
blended with ice in a glass.

Now it's all I can do to look at them
plump in the store, remembering
how in our cleanest clothes we wept in corners
at having to give her up,
for she meant to change the world.

Weeks she held out
scoured hollow with unslakeable thirst which
I imagined carmine,

and at the kitchen sink I ground and re-ground ice
to cool the mouth so dry it withered
half the words she would have said,

leaving *thirsty*
leaving *won't be long now*
leaving *take some of me into your life*

Last Day

Before my shift we dug a small white birch
into the corner of the front yard
as sentinel, I thought,
giving up on luck and any version of bargain.

Through the day she held my hand,
flicked her nail at the spots of paint
that escaped the fence she had sent me to
in her way of dispersing friends to business
she was concluding.

By turns we stirred the chipped ice,
I read her a letter from the stash she kept close on the bed,
mostly she rode the pain.
I'm going on, she said before the men came home
and she turned what little she had toward teasing.

At seven I left,
closing the house into a further stillness.
So like the dawn the colours of the evening
often are with the same pale announcement.

Because this is November,
the poplars at the lake point their dead-end
limbs up, abbreviated lopsided versions
of themselves, against a sky of smoke and fire.

Because it is November, men in bright vests
with guns stalk the woods — glad no doubt
for few leaves and broken trees,
the better no doubt to find the prey.

Around the cabin two hounds sniff,
small gold bells around their necks
make them into seasonal ornaments
instead of hunting dogs, and they look as though they know it.

Here I have finally to understand that what for most of my life
I believed to be grief turns out not to be — sorrow for the deer,
for the trees, even for the friend, not sadness at all,
nothing to do with the tolling of the bell of the heart,

betrayal, abandonment, all the paraphernalia of loss
done up like a Greek play, and all the time plain old rage,
which seems a disgrace, somehow, unworthy in these
times when the days leak heat and the hard season leans in, but
listen —

once revealed, there is no compromise,
rage burns the insides out of surrender,
makes you crave the moon food water sun,
makes you starved for everything.

Fatou Dust: Lament for a Mother

for Sally Sharpe

1. Tuesday: Naomi

With the shape of the question round as sleep
I want to know why, light and unaccountable,
a small piece of coral loosens itself,
falls away in a tidebreath —
the return voyage,
a weight borne by the world entire.

The child is dead.
Fastened to the seabed,
the sorrowing reef remains.

2. The Book of Ruth

Impossible to absorb
this unspeakable reversal.

Now it came to pass when judges ruled,
the hours lay like dead crows,
dull, broken by this undoing.

The daughter has issued the mother
into a purification; blank, roaring.

Now it came to pass there was a famine
in the land and a flood,
and the mother was capsized,
filled with unleashed livid water:
urgent   shapeless   twisting
pressing.

And all that the people could say was:
we are witnesses.

3. What Ruth Got Left With

Every day a scuffed cart hauls her raddled
heart along a back road,
beyond civil limits and reasonable safety
to the disposal site,
so she may gaze for as long as she is able
at items of abandonment

junked by a previous owner,
who happened to be her daughter.

Brown-edged guesswork,
salvage limited to pieces of paper.
If this is fiction the plot stinks,
if this is a story it's a short one,
its chapters become waste.

Whither thou goest not an idle question.
No amount of cheap travel time
will get her there.
She has turned up at the wrong end of the harvest.
The reaper has come
and gone.

4. For the Siblings of Suicides Who Feel the Guilt of Failed Love

What else do you need to know
about choosing to die?

Inventory:

stopped clock,
a row of empties, zero which is not the same as nothing left to live for,

how you will get left with the mess
       the heaved stones of it
       piled in front of you,
       behind.

The thing I hate most about suicide (you say)
is the lack of connection it reveals,
and I have to say that what I hate most
is its wholesale trade in ash and ruined faces,
how they are lined up in the rearview mirror
trying to commit the rules of the road to memory
from a book that never got written.

5. Six Months On

After the bird hits the glass only the smallest
movement of muscles and bone betray life.

*the street
does not hold
the sky*

The sum of the known
history disassembles on impact.

*coastlines
cannot be
measured*

The mother sits in her room off the front hall by
the door to the street, barrenness incarnate,
by her beating heart the content of the sea is erased.

*cycles
indefinitely**

Books on shelves and fragments.
Later she will go out and walk familiar streets.
No one can know what she sees.

dust **

* "At this point the behaviour of the dynamical system becomes chaotic
jumping around all over the place for no apparent reason."
(*Mathematics: the New Golden Age*, Keith Devlin, Penguin, 1988. pg. 90)

** "Here infinity is the only attractor, and the Julia set dissolves
into isolated points called *Fatou dust*." Ibid, pg. 98.

6. Anniversary

we hauled her things up from cellar storage this
morning
my daughter is a bunch of cartons
she says
as we pass one another in the upstairs
hall
the daughter is also two brown bags of
ashes
on the top shelf downstairs in the room by
the door
hear the mother's words: *Child it's been a*
year
in this devastation the pain is outrageous   May you be
held
in the arms of Infinity   And I will see you again

tonight
she takes the lids off the boxes holds up one by
one
the painted jeans and the tiny fish earring
teddybear
knapsack and one crumpled black shoe then its
mate
the house pressing varnished wood around us
corridors
without windows   the tyranny of this ferocious

night

    stretched on a blackened leather sea   o god

if the trumpet

    shall sound and the dead be raised incorruptible

lift the child

    who died by her own hand in her fourteenth year

7. "The Great Disorder We Have Encountered"

Imagine how to put in the rest of your life.
Watch the parts fly whirl crack off other pieces.
Ambush is everywhere.
It is spring. All the leaves are falling from the trees.
There will be no atonement.

8. Prayer

Make of her
groundwater,
the outer edge of castled ice
lit by sun.
Let her disappear
among jasper touchstones.
Sink her through brindled prairie grass
to a beneath
where she may lie
ten thousand years.
Preserve her all her loves
in inextinguishable aerial music
for this aquafied hereafter.

Dialogue:
Zero Which is not the Same as Nothing

for, and with, Joan Geramita

When the dialogue opens, the mathematician is in one city, separated from family and friends by 300 kilometres, exploring ways in which mathematical choice influences political decisions. The poet is in the-family-and-friends-city writing and recovering from cancer. And then, in the middle of winter, a young girl kills herself.

THE POET

This is a cold day draped in blue shadow. A friend's child has committed suicide. She was thirteen. I go every morning to help paint her room yellow, golden, the colour that passes for hope. We drink cups of tea until we taste only bitterness. At dusk we wash the rollers and brushes and cups. This is all that anyone can think to do.

I watch the aftermath of this death. Casual activity is out of the question. Yet what I do, however considered, lacks meaning. My natural urges freeze in this abyss where everyone has been yanked into pain. No one sleeps. A minute becomes the weight of one empty day succeeding another. Each person gagged and bound to the end of love.

How can I understand? The resounding *Yes* that cancer taught me has become a sound in a foreign tongue, useless against this howl of annihilation. As I write I want urgency to burn in my words. Instead they are blurred, drab, witless.

Suicide is not a standstill, a conclusion. Nor can it be turned inside out into an elegy, revealing the wonder of living by way of its rejection. Choosing to die is never the slate wiped clean, because suicide is not a solo. It is a drama with a cast of players, a series with endless reruns. Listen, everything I see convinces me of suicide's treachery, its mess of bystanders forever cornered. Such deaths are permanent contusions — pools of blood never to be absorbed.

One day you were going to talk to me about numbers. I wish you would. I imagine solace in them, in what they can do. Just now I like the idea of you sitting in a room thinking about numbers.

THE MATHEMATICIAN

You aren't the first to tell me of this death. My daughter who goes to school with her brother, called me. I am reminded of course of my own brother, one who also chose to die.

It is interesting that you imagine solace in numbers or in thinking about them. The Pythagoreans used numbers as a fundamental model of the world, considered that they captured the essence of things, both those we see and those we don't. A kind of atomic theory. When a new kind of number was discovered (the irrational number, so called because it is not the ratio of whole numbers), it precipitated a theological crisis of sorts. For them, to think about numbers was to think about the nature of the universe.

I don't give numbers such a fundamental role. But even for me, they are far more than just the name of an amount. Taken together they are an idea but they are also individual entities. Each number contains within itself other numbers and relationships, like those Russian nesting dolls, or those wooden puzzles people sometimes keep on their coffee tables or like beehives or families. For example, even numbers are able to decompose into two equal parts that add up to the original number, like 12 is 6 + 6. The odd numbers, of course, can't do this equal decomposition thing. I always see them as having a hook out ready to catch onto another odd number.

The addition of two odd numbers produces an even number which in my mind is smooth like an egg with no one part of it more interesting than another (until of course you — or the creature within — crack it open). There is something about the process of odd numbers combining and losing their oddness and their external distinction and becoming egg-like and only internally intricate that is a koan for me and I imagine that I understand the reverence the Pythagoreans had for numbers.

*

For me reverence means paying attention to the details of living, the slivers and parings and chunks: bridges, oatmeal, intersections, the iris, whispers. I don't ruminate about what existence means, or where my place in it lies, because I'm busy watching. It's not that I trust sight more than thinking; more that I am swept up by the rumpus into which my senses deliver me, merciless and excessive. I only have to open one eye in the morning and it begins. Hello. Welcome. Look how light hits the wall. Do you hear music? There is ice in the trees. You had better get going. Or, you could lie here for a while and feel the flannel sheets against your skin. What's it to be?

I want to examine the world one piece at a time, not once but over and over, until the pieces become a track to the purity which is beyond words and feelings. Not to be called away from the livid moment but to travel to its storm centre, to climb into Pandora's box, container of life and death, which is in the end empty.

Being as egocentric as anyone else, my assumption is that this bedazzlement with living is universal, that you too, for example, find yourself captured by the world through the body, are ground and polished by the sentient. I figure that everyone watches as carefully as I do, gives as little attention to the job of the head: naming the meaning.

*

But you give lots of attention to the job of the head! What is a poem, after all, if not the consequence of ruminations on the interplay of watcher and watched, an attempt to express the meaning gleaned by one person at least? A poem is definition, theorem and proof all in one.

*

It's an attempt only, like trying to assign words to the toenail on the back leg of the proverbial elephant. Didn't you once say that poems were akin to posing questions in math, that is, you really don't ask the question until you know the answer? I see the similarity but in the case of poems, the answer is fabricated out of instinct to capture, and out of love for words.

For me, the body — its mileage of tissue and bone and cartilage, its oceans of water, its occupation of laying down notations of experience as intricate as wave theory — is a tumble of miracles. One miracle (we had better allow miracles because we are bound to run up against rules) must be the way this universe of thought and sensation, its brushed pulse, is gathered up, gathered in without indentation or crack — entire — in moments of blind joy or sudden insight, the way in which you can solve a puzzle, quickly, without knowing where the answer came from.

Obviously I'm making a case that tries to be analogous to your even numbers, not because I want to suggest a reckless devotion to experience, but I find myself full of Pythagorean awe, and its source is available to all: being alive. Which is why I have so much trouble understanding this child's suicide, any suicide. Who could opt for zero and miss one second? No, not zero, zero at least relates to one and three. Oblivion. Nothing. What is nothing, why choose it?

*

You are right, of course, zero and nothing are not the same. I seem to remember that once you wanted a discussion on the difference between zero and nothing. I offer the discussion now, as a space-maker, a place-holder as it were, while I too grapple with the reverberations of choosing nothing.

You actually have the essence of it. Zero is the number-name given to the amount "nothing." It is also the boundary between the positive and negative numbers, a resting-place, a balance point. It is also a numeral which permits us to write numbers conveniently by taking up space without filling it. Zero is what lets us tell the difference between a "1 in the ten's position" and a "1 in the unit's position" between 10 and 1. Nothing, on the other hand, is nothing, unless, I think, you are a Buddhist, in which case it is also everything.

*

Or a quaker, wherein it releases silence into illumination.

I must tell you about a meeting house in Maryland, Old Third Haven, established about 1682, over the bridge from Annapolis. We found it last summer. The old frame building had twelve-paned windows, its several green doors thrown open to let out the urge to speech and let in a stillness as elderly as trees. The floorboards were a foot wide, scarred. Between them lay shale tamped down, trod upon, swept clean as plainsong. The benches sloped back, prepared to wait. Over them dust, hung in triangled light struts, assumed no pattern. The building was plain. The elaboration lay in the harmony of its dimensions. It was as though proportion had laid siege to the situation.

At the threshold in falling light, I felt emptiness stretched before me in accord with what happens in times of sudden loss. The sun-shafted silence was at odds with sensations of motion. Beams cracked as they will in cold and heat: the smack of axe into original growth. Glass in the windowpanes rippled in disturbance. The rafters held exact angles; the windows were rectangles within rectangles, parallel planked floorboards an exercise in perspective. Geometry, here, held the past in check. Walls and floor gave off the smell of a granary: oats and small rodents by night. It took me over — suddenly and completely — the way fear of dying has.

I draw out this description because shape and silence seemed to draw attention to themselves, even announced themselves, as though offering a certain presentiment of events the building had witnessed — rapture, quick fevers, unexplained birth, sudden death by hanging — through bare essentials. No distractions, nothing, everything.

*

Death by hanging. I know you want a respite but I find I really must return to suicide. My brother was 25 when he hanged himself and I was 22. It was a choice so totally unacceptable in my family that we never spoke of it. But this silence left his choice unchallenged. You seem so sure, so clear on the awfulness of suicide but it has turned up on my list of "possibles."

This past fall I spent some days acutely aware that the suffering of the innocent is intrinsic to the smooth running of the world. I did (and do) realize that death is a requirement for life, but, it appeared to me that, in addition, during life evil actually has the upper hand. In that case, it is far from obvious that living is preferable to not living. I was in a world where to live is to be powerless and complicit in the evil that surrounds us.

The argument goes like this. Humans require adversity to grow in essential ways. Unable to be both mature and innocent we actually require encounters with evil to reach our full potential.

Why agree to such rules? It is not as if success were guaranteed. Some humans are destroyed in this regime. We find their souls on the slag heap produced by torturers or those principled persons who consider human suffering a required subject in life's hard school. Indeed, a rational consideration of the situation leads to the conclusion that the only way to "win" in this uneven contest is to refuse to "play."

Why is suicide so awful? A successful culture must balance a genetically supported prohibition of suicide (at least until the young are on their way) against a societal requirement in favour of suicide in support of the group. We call it love of country or loyalty to principle or obedience to god. We award medals and fancy funerals and we threaten shame and disgrace to those who would save themselves at the expense of their comrades. But when suicide supports only the individual then it must be denounced as evil and irrational, unhuman.

Tell me about your technicolour world, awash in possibility and promise. Explain to me how the good times can be worth it when they rely on the suffering of others. Tell me how to live, not in the face of death, but in the face of evil. Is my black view an aberration to be challenged or just another way to see the world? Am I deaf and blind? Or are you? Or are you deaf while I am blind?

*

Existence in which suffering is essential to the running of the world, smoothly or roughly, where evil prevails — this is your world. I don't know it. Or rather, mine differs. In mine, good times exist alongside suffering; good times are part of the world, as is suffering, indifference, cruelty, craving, music, insects, forks, northern lights, highways, even suicide.

I am beginning to wonder why I can't make you see this as a fascinating array. You wonder about my hearing. It may be that I can't bear to think about you suffering the suffering of others, can't bear the conclusion this might lead you to, and so I choose what I hear.

You see, I felt sure that I could make the case for life with pictures, evoke technicolour by way of black and white words, state purely, with unusual appeal, how I find living in the world miraculous. I would give you this brilliant alpha-omega jumble in irrefutable descriptions. You would come to understand the folly of thinking you have to choose between death and life after I had convinced you that living, if not always enchanting, is various, and can be shot through with joy. Then, in that moment, you would have it for your own. In that instant you would be safe. Which of course is not possible, safety is not possible and anyway, how can I presume to ask you to surrender your own logic to my persuasions? (How can I not?)

What I can't imagine, however hard I try, is what sort of experience, what pain or linked association of thought, propels a person to a resolve to end life. Lots of people find life bleak but they don't consider suicide. How does deciding to die happen?

*

How does deciding to die happen? I only know what I have sifted from my own experience and my brother's. He died without a word of explanation; perhaps he never meant to die, planned to explain afterwards; if so, a bad miscalculation.

It seems to me there are many ways to end up considering suicide. Here are two separate reflections that lead there. One centres on the question: Do I wish to continue to participate in this existence as I know it? (If the answer is no, change or end this existence...) The other centres on the question: What is the point of this existence as I know it? It is a search for meaning in the universe, for the meaning of the individual life. It is hard to get people to give you enough space to work on this question. Other things intrude, like shovelling snow…Unless of course, you can convince them that it is important, maybe even a matter of life and death and the fact is you have to convince yourself of that as well. Part of the enterprise becomes a search for words, metaphors, symbols to express the depth and importance of the work. It is hard to wander in this blighted landscape, profoundly unhappy, taken care of by others. Being willing to die underlines the importance of the work, allows it to continue. Suicide can be a way to say THIS IS REALLY IMPORTANT, I'M NOT KIDDING, THIS STUFF MATTERS ENOUGH FOR ME TO DIE FOR IT.

It would be good if those who wander in those places realized that we do not have to risk death in order to think these thoughts.

*

I picture you writing away, risking life to think about death, light blazing from your head like a medieval saint. You make it sound as though everybody now and then thinks about suicide when she isn't concerned about snow removal or groceries. I don't buy it.

I understand your first reflection in the usual way: a person takes a look around and decides not to participate in existence as he or she knows it. I believe this happens, although I can't imagine doing so myself, and I wonder: is this a failure of my imagination? Hard as I try, recalling as I do the abject terror into which cancer hurled me, I fail to find any picture of existence unbearable enough to warrant me chucking it. Not even to avoid certain deaths I have witnessed and fear might one day be mine: alone, in uncontrolled pain.

Which brings me smack up against the second enterprise: what is the point of existence? Is the point of existence the same for you as for me? If I tell you the meaning of existence, is my conclusion true?

*

I haven't been clear enough. The truth of your conclusion doesn't matter. What matters is that you take seriously my question and are willing to engage in a discussion about the issue. I think that it is very hard to live with someone who is wrestling with this question. And I think a lot of people don't want to think about this question and have little patience with those of us who do —

*

Or are scared out of their minds —

*

Maybe scared too. In any case, here would be this person, apparently moping around, going on about the meaning of existence and the general screwed-up-ed-ness of the universe and the people he was living with would be unaware, or uninterested or impatient —

*

Or scared out of their minds —

*

Scared of what? Scared that somebody dares to think about this question? Scared that perhaps they will have to think about this stuff too? Fed up more likely, fed up with the gloom and separation the thinker is radiating, especially if the driveway needs shovelling or something like that. And the "thinker" might well share the view that her preoccupation was self-indulgent or frivolous (especially if there are kids to feed...) unless perhaps it really were a question of existence — surely that would be important enough to spend time on —

*

Yes —

*

And so one thinks — I thought — of suicide — or the risk of suicide — as a way to verify mostly for myself the importance of what I was thinking about, a way to prove to myself that I was seriously engaged here and not just posturing. (You might like to know that I found this argument, once I had deciphered it, absurd. For me, absurd is good as an antidote to suicide.)

I don't think my brother did this, by the way. I've come to think he wanted to ask for help and had no words (another route to that consideration). But there was no warning (that I could read) and I'll never know.

*

Yes, we do dismiss each other's words and behaviours out of irritation, out of anger, out of self-centredness. People may appear indifferent or disengaged because they are cautious or uncaring. However, in my experience, the overriding emotion is fear. Knowing someone who might be at risk of suicide is terrifying and indescribably worse if you love her. What may appear to be indifference could be an attempt not to escalate the situation, could be denial, could be sheer paralysis.

What good are you dead? What good to anybody? You have answered your question about the meaning of the individual life with a resounding *Nothing*! What can that mean to the people left? Does the tackling of existential questions — after the fact — remain brave and if so, of what value is its bravery to those who live on with such a legacy?

What cross-purposes we appear to be at. You want me to understand the pain of the thinker. It's the possible consequence of this thinker's "thinking" that makes me wild. I want you to tell me how the bystander can stop the thinker, to hell with reason and never mind the pain, because the conundrum has everything at stake. I want to take your quest and heave it in the river. There. Have done with it. Heartbreak is not permitted. I want to drag you to a pond full of marsh marigolds and have you consider the qualities of green and gold for a full day. There, live for green and gold. For ponds. For water.

*

Yes, that's exactly it. I want you to understand the pain of the thinker. I want you to understand what it would cost the thinker to alleviate the bystander's fear.

Remember the even numbers? The numbers which can be divided into two equal parts? Powers of 2 are the ultimate in even numbers, they can be divided into two equal parts and then each of those (2) parts can be divided into two equal parts and then each of those (4) parts can be divided into two equal parts. As an example: 1,073,741,824 is the thirtieth power of 2; that is, when we multiply 2 times itself 30 times we get 1,073,741,824. The thirtieth power of two is written 2^{30}. Anyway, if you start with 2^{30} you can keep on halving it until at last you have the number divided into 536,970,912 equal parts (each part is a 2). Now of course if you divide all those 2's in half, you end up with only 1's, 1,073,741,824 of them. We have magically moved from new information — 2^{30} can be written as the sum of 2 equal parts, of 4 equal parts...up to a sum of 536,870,912 equal parts, to: not-new information — 2^{30} can be written as the sum of 1,073,741,824 equal parts which you knew from the start because among its many meanings 1,073,741,824 means the sum of that many 1's.

Imagine being in a world where sadness is raised to a very high power. It smothers you. When you try to sort things out, analyze your situation, get a grip on something, anything — you find that you are grabbing at more copies of the original, smaller perhaps but not essentially different. The process is rather like dividing a power of 2 in half. How much of an improvement is it to replace 2^{30} by two copies of 2^{29}? ($2^{30} = 2^{29} + 2^{29}$). Imagine if you will, in this sea of identical egg-shaped sadnesses, gently rocking to and fro, a path that winds among them. Would it not be enticing? Might you not follow it? Despair is that path. It seizes the attention like a streak of scarlet in a sea of grey, offering respite from the din and the possibility of order. Despair eliminates the clutter, quiets the clamour, simplifies the choices, offers a single well-defined solution.

And the bystanders are very far away — being terrified.

*

Great the danger, that distance! How does the bystander travel through it? And far greater the danger when the live-or-die preoccupation remains hidden, when the despair is invisible, inaudible. Who can counter what she does not suspect?

And how do you counter that kind of despair anyway? That's what I want to know. What words penetrate a closed system? How is a person supposed to make someone else understand that the beauty of one gesture can cancel an act of betrayal, if that person believes evil holds the upper hand and good times rely on suffering? All the brilliance of the world must fail against such an All Or Nothing. Here's the point: there has to be an argument to prove the bleak world deficient. It is what the bystander needs, the bystander who has little room for debate because she is incapacitated with terror and running out of time.

*

In the end, the choice is the chooser's to make and the responsibility for the choice is the chooser's.

You started out by asking how a person might come to consider suicide. My response really deals with coming to the point of considering suicide; it doesn't address what makes a person willing to consider the option of suicide for longer than it takes to say *No*. As you say, life is bleak for lots of people and most of them appear not to consider suicide as a solution.

I think that — in the end — the decision about suicide depends on how well the decider sees the bystanders. It depends on whether the decider sees herself connected to other people enough that she can see their pain as well as her own and is willing to endure her pain to spare them theirs. It depends on whether the glimpses of green and gold are at least as enticing as the path through the ever-replicating sadness.

It depends on being able to see the green and gold at all.

II
Green and Gold

The temple bell stops
and the sound keeps coming
out of the flowers.

— BASHO

As Lines, so Loves oblique may well
Themselves in every Angle greet:
But ours so truly Parallel,
Though infinite can never meet.

— ANDREW MARVELL

Codex on Flight

To set down what happened plainly is what she wants.

First she thought to give the story from the point of view of a Renaissance genius. Someone of consequence.

So she lost herself in the great metal tongues of abbey bells and the politics of Tuscany. She reviewed the furnishings of Lorenzo di Medici's bedchamber, pursued the history of map-making. She spun each into an explanation, turned the explanation toward coincidence, tried to press coincidence into wisdom. Or acceptance. Now she knows better.

It turns out that the only point of view she has is her own.

As you will see, the other story is his.

Leonardo da Vinci completed his *Codex on the Flight of Birds* at Florence, in 1505. He studied the problem of flight for many years, beginning in Milan, in 1483, continuing until his death, in voluntary exile in France. The *Codex* takes its place among his notes, drawings, and other manuscripts on this subject.

Anchino, near Vinci
April 15, 1452

Born toward midnight nearby: Leonardo,
bastard son to Piero da Vinci, notary public,
        bocco, a mouth to feed,
to Catarina,
to the lime-burner *Accattabriga* (the Quarreler)
to Francesco, uncle
to the slopes of Monte Albano
to darting streams
to tiny fields worked bent-backed with mattocks
to poppies and mulberry
to cypress
to ancient olives trimmed as goblets
to occasional oyster shells nearby in marshes
to weather and plants
to solitude
to riddles
to numbers
to the Deluge
to exile
to legend.

Tilt

I knelt by the hole in the ice, turned your face to me, your lips to my
hand. Cold arose and settled in my skin like water into pumice.
Colour departed. I remained there all night,
even though they had taken
you away.

At times like this they say it will get easier. They say
numbness is a blessing. They say at least
it was quick. They say the innocent are
spared the grief of the world. They say
don't forget you have the others.
They say there are worse
things. They say you
shouldn't blame
yourself. They
say time will
heal. They
say you
have to
live
on.

Porta San Friano, Florence
February 19, 1469

Leonardo waits the pleasure
of the salt-tax inspector,
he is bound for the Via dello Pretanza
where his father rents rooms,
Ser Piero, procurator of the Cloister,
agent and financial manager for the monks of San Donato.

He is apprenticed to the studio of Verrocchio,
goldsmith, where he decorates chests
paints banners
gilds baskets
eats pasta and drinks wine
makes death masks and completes
the work of the other apprentices
at the kiln turntable easel and workbench.

Leonardo crosses Porte alla Carraia,
leans against a whitewashed wall
to inscribe the story of a bird he has just remembered
in his notebook:

To write thus clearly about the kite
would seem to be my fate, because in the earliest
recollections of my infancy it seemed to me
that when I was in the cradle, a kite
came down and opened my mouth with its tail,
and struck me within upon the lips with
its tail many times.

He is seventeen.

Situated

Perhaps this is where the story should open, here, today.

Winter dirt sheens each pane. The rooms remain sealed. It's too cold
to wash windows. Meantime there's silver to polish. Mrs. Nakamura
loves hers. She travels to London's Silver Vaults each spring.
She buys Thread and Shell, fills the mahogany sideboard with blue felt
cloths pocketed for knives and forks, sacked for candlesticks. The carving
set lies in an oak box. There are grape scissors, nutcrackers, a spooner.
Mrs. Nakamura wants them seen to regularly. She entertains.

Mrs. Mullock would forget she had silver if I didn't remind her. She says
it belongs in the ground. I take her to mean that she'd return the cutlery
to ore if she could, not that it was ill-gotten, though judging from the
stories she tells about her late husband, either could be true. She tells me
silver is captured and should be released. I humour her because, as a
matter of fact, I know what she means. Her kids collect stainless, those
that collect. One of them prefers renunciation, like his mother.
His renunciation is sweeping, however, and includes Mrs. Mullock.

Some people swear by liquid dip. Myself I like the white paste
and a hank of flannelette. Fill the sink with soapy water. Apply
the polish. Do a few at a time or the paste will dry. Rubbing brings
satisfaction, reveals the shine.

Lost in a border, following a pattern, I think I am black in the creases
from exposure. Certainly I lack lustre. I ought to brighten but it may
always be too soon. Or too late.

If you are bothered by tarnish, remember it is only surface film.

Florence
May 1, 1471

From the records:
Dancers with garlands, solutions of gilt:
Verrocchio is Pageant-Master.

Lorenzo di Medici rides with trumpeters
and tabourers and fifers.
His plumed horse is white
his gown is red and white silk with hems of pearls,
on his shield a kingly diamond,
torch bearers in emerald
silver falcon feathers scattered in their cloaks.

The feast
which is seven hours long:
after each course the silver plates
will be thrown from the window
to guarantee clean dishes,
and the court jester will entertain
by sucking four hundred eggs and eating
a camel hair coat; after almond and marrow soup,
young Leonardo will have imperial eagles in sugar,
gilded oranges and capons in parsley sauce,
geese peacocks lamb rabbit pheasant deer,
and conclude with ices marzipan.

Verrocchio will return to the studio
to complete preparations
for hoisting the great gilt ball and cross
(2 tons, 6 metres wide) designed by Brunelleschi
to the tower of the Santa Maria del Fiore.

Force

On the subway I write rules to live by in my notebook. I revise them as circumstances change.

1. I will rely on the obligation of touch.

2. In certain situations running away becomes honourable.

3. Where there are rules, a person will discover exceptions.

All my life I've been undercover. I wear the habit of the ordinarily nice, the cloak of the exceptionally thoughtful, a disguise of the apparently open-and-attuned-to-others, as though these bits of cloth could fool catastrophe right out of the picture.

For years it has been necessary to conceal me further, even from myself. There seemed no choice. It happened suddenly, in the instant, like fine rain where there was no rain, and the picture of me blurred. Now, to myself, I am the not-very-smart who can therefore be excused from understanding, the accepting person who wants next to nothing.

Most of the time this works. By day the ruse takes care of itself. Expecting little removes the sting of anticipation. Wanting nothing leaves just what happens. The trouble starts at the end of the day, arriving as a voice. Night, a black onslaught, rips the camouflage away. Down to the skin and listening, this is when leave-taking must be considered.

Day of St. Mary of the Snows
August 5, 1473

In the upper left corner
of the yellow-tinted paper,
Leonardo writes the date
in perfect reverse script,

then below draws his pen lightly
laterally, the merest horizon,
dropping next to graze the planes of fields,
raises high hills to the right
and with a young lover's touch stretches
lake water taut with quick lateral strokes
not unlike those of the Japanese master
'Toyo Sesshu.

A fleet of boats with a single turning stroke,
trees gestures of wind,
cliffs impatiently shadowed.

Hatched into the foreground
a river pours its livid weight
over the rockface in line after audacious line.

No figures mar the tension of rocks and water,
no bird in the shimmering air.
This is his first known landscape.
Leonardo is twenty-one.
Has the painter found his beloved?

Where shall I take my place?

Wind

I cling to one end of a lost love.

Flying in the unbearable loneliness of the last of the curlew
flying to you over the black spruce forest
in green opalescence
crangs and moss and dovekies hummocked on seacliffs
over pyrite and mica
muskeg ponds
purple crowberries of the Ungava

through the twilight on the back of the humpbacked whale
eyes of a seal hang in the sky like preserved amber
flying to touch the nape of your neck
cold skin
with the golden plovers by the perilous sea route.

Over Lancaster Sound
candle ice clattering to shards
pack ice calving beneath me
I am the light flying to you
your burden of cold
white heart held long at the northwest passage.

The Studio, Florence
February 3, 1475

This day it is thought
that Leonardo may have posed
for Verrocchio's David,
leaning his body into bronze.

It is said that Leonardo's beauty
lay in the silence at the heart of music,
that he studied mirrors, dipped a lizard
in quicksilver, kept it tame in a box,

that his lute was wood ornamented with roses
shaped to a horse's head,
its music the deferred inheritance
of wind.

To understand the intersection of waves
he examined the scales of fir cones,
and watched closely the descent of butterflies
against the damp vapour of dawn air.

At the end of his life
he would make for the King of France
a mechanical lion whose chest opened
revealing a garden filled with lapis lilies,

and that at his death would be found
among his papers in another's hand,
ink-stained, scarcely legible:
My Leonardo, why dost thou so torment me?

Arc of the Circle

In all honesty clearing up after people is what's left for me. I work
without bustle, with care. I keep equipment to a minimum. Bucket, mop,
cloths. I charge the going rate. Trustworthy and quiet, after landing
the first job the others fell in my lap.

Cleaning allows most of me to vanish, except for my hands. The one
indulgence I allow myself is to observe what is beautiful. I have
a good eye.

Throughout my houses I am dustless and mirrored, washed and folded.
By noon I am undeniably clean. By three I have become a Wilton carpet,
flocked wallpaper, a piece of Steuben crystal, two ermine incised
within. Or a rare Ozias Leduc landscape, maples decanting shadows
on cream and sugar snow. Pigment, glass. You can imagine.

Such retreat never lasts. Usually by late afternoon an insistence, barely
audible, unbuckles itself from the silence, a small collection of words
such as old prayers require: *yes, you are buried here*. That's just what
I want, I say to the room.

Each day loneliness takes me to the horizon which moves ahead like
coastline. Each week doubles back on the one before. I like the curve
of repetition.

Office of the Bight and Monasteries
April 9, 1476

Anonymous charges dropped into the drum
Buchi della Verita (mouths of Truth)
concerning the boy model presumed
the angel at the right hand of Christ
in the baptismal scene
luminous skin silken curls
golden halo and a cross-eyed
angel in his arms, no wings.

Awaiting trial
Leonardo occupies himself
perfecting a hieroglyphic
signature, draws a knot made
so that the cord
may be traced from one end
to the other the whole
filling a round space.

He loves all animals,
trains them with gentleness,
possesses little, works seldom,
keeps horses and servants
the latter of which he is fond.
Conditional discharge —
absoluti cum conditione ut retamburenntur
(brought back to the drum) tried again:
charges dropped.

Pray hold me not in scorn!
Do you answer for yourself!

Distance Between

I should tell you how my day goes. In the morning I clean. Usually
at noon I shop on the main street in this cold city. I'm left a list. Today
there's Murphy soap and vinegar, boneless chicken breasts, and apples
for Mrs. Nakamura.

The Chinese greengrocer and I understand one another. Apples by
the kilo, he says. Happiness by the back door, I reply as he hands me
the bag. We are slips of paper falling out of fortune cookies. I carry
the parcel as though it were full of crystal hearts that might break
without careful handling.

Apples grew beside the house. Apples, pasture rose and wild grape. Even
as a baby, eating wasn't something you were ever interested
in. Or sleeping. You wanted only apple juice and activity. From
the minute you learned to stand you wanted out, outside, to be
on your way.

Afterward they told me not to make any sudden changes in my life.
I could have died laughing. As if, as if a person could even chew or
swallow.

If I believed in angels I'd hire one to reel you in.

Tuscany, eclipse of the sun
October 14, 1478

Outside the city of the Red Lily
palaces of pleasure: loggia, tunnels of pleached
and knotted trees, oleander, grottoes of cypress.

Inside the city behold the age of despots
and artisans: coffered roofs, Etruscan stone,
friezes, cornices, portals, market stalls,
straw-covered cobblestones where the painter
pursues the secrets of material powders:

> ashes of emery beaten by hammers
> enamel dissolved in tartar yields blue
> brass vitrified gives red
> Star of Bethlehem flower.

Against a creamy wall the goldfinch,
its foot lightly chained to a metal perch,
plumed emblem of chaste love
purchased and returned to freedom.

All afternoon the painter draws draperies
for a kneeling figure, inky fingers
dusted with white chalk.

Which is better — to draw from nature
or from the antique?
And which is more difficult
— the lines or the light and shade?

Leonardo remodels his reputation.

Wishes to Rise

I remember nothing of the day after, or the week. There might
have been a blizzard. Friends brought food. They came with empty
boxes that they took away full. Words filled rooms. Each day
a wind roared through the city bending trees, galed around me,
tumbling the words and cards, casseroles and flowers.

The first year became the second, then the third. We lived in an afterward
unrolling from a circle in the middle of winter. No one dared remember
before. What were my feelings? Might better ask a wrecked building.
What did I think about? Frankly for a long stretch I fought to not
think at all.

Four years along I moved out and started cleaning. The others were
relieved, I think; released.

Andean women took spindles to the grave. I plan to take my cloths:
swathes of soft cotton, gauze for chrome, strips of sheets, torn silk
for polishing enamel, linen shirt sleeves for brass, chamois, organza,
georgette. I wish to be fabric. I will work hard, and then become
transparent, at last unravelling into threads in the wind.
Become airborne.

Duomo, December 28, 1479

The Plot: The state of the church envelops the state
of Florence. Alliances shift, Lorenzo di Medici
enters into talks with Venice and Milan, to
safeguard the peace, he says. The Pope and the
Archbishop of Pisa make arrangements. At the
tinkling of the mass bell, at the solemn elevation
of the Host, under the cupola by Brunelleschi, the
assassins strike —

one Medici sinks,
Lorenzo escapes. Beautiful brother at the altar,
his robes a pool of purple blood.

Drama of the betrayal puts one killer on the roof
deafened by the great metal tongues of the bells
then fleeing on foot, returned from the Bosporus
in chains, hanged at the Palazzo del Capitano,
sketched by Leonardo at the gallows
with exquisite care to detail:

> six buttons/ fur-lined overcloak
> small bonnet/ hollow-eyed/ tight-jawed.

Let the movements of men be such as are in
keeping with their dignity or meanness.

On the body of the other, Old Jacobo,
street urchins perpetrate unspeakable atrocities,
toss his body into the Arno where it floats
downstream under the bridge at Pisa
slowly out to sea.

Trifles

Mrs. Mullock's asked me to take another house, a friend down the street.
I have enough work as it is, but I can't say no to her. This is only one
of my problems.

He lives alone and teaches, religion maybe, something along those lines.
I call him Scholar, not to his face. He's tidy, which is lucky, and leaves
for the day when I arrive. He's not used to having anyone in the house
with him. Turns out the place is stark, not much in the way of furniture,
so I finish quickly.

In the afternoon I sit in his study by the west window so I'll catch
a glimpse of him coming around the corner on his way home. The walls
are shelved except for the door and window. There are other things besides
books, a mauve rock, amethyst, I think, a hunk of concrete with a small
brass plate screwed into it, *Berlin Wall*. Taking care not to touch
anything, I read book titles and look at the paintings tacked to
the shelving uprights. There must be twenty of them, all small, old
paintings of angels. I like the backgrounds, mountains mostly, or stone
hill cities.

The roundabout route home from the subway takes me past stores full
of leather, linens, ivory, fur. I'm planning a lawn sale, a renunciation.
The time has arrived to surrender the photographs and the drawings of
icebergs and glaciers, if only because I want to keep them. I've had
discussions of this sort with myself every day for two years. If I
recognize this as necessary — and I do — then I ought to be able to find
a way to make myself do it.

Corte Vecchia, Milan
April 23, 1485

New city, new start.
Leonardo receives a commission,
a Nativity to be sent to Matthias Corvinus,
makes notes to himself:

Talk about the sea with the man from Genoa,

...because however far the eyes
of the navigators carried by ships
may move through the universe
they behold at the same time
the image of the sun through
all the waters of their hemisphere
in all the movements
made in all aspects...

He is lonely
does not drink
eats sparingly
begins the clay model
for the equestrian statue
that will be known
as The Great Horse,

bewitches brass
into a series of navigational instruments
kept by the bedside of Ludovico Maria Sforza Anglo,
Il Moro, Duke of Milan.

Impact

Memory lays traps. Even avoiding mirrors and most music, I am turned
to stone by a trace scent: wet wool, orange peel, toast. Some memories,
on the other hand, work like sandpaper on rough edges.

One year the lake froze to unusual depths. Shore ice threw itself up in
a jagged blue wall along the waterfront. Wind ground ice against itself,
the scarifying heard for blocks. The ferry ploughed back and forth to
the island, the only open water for miles. Then, thaw. The temperature
shot up. I kidnapped a friend late one afternoon. We went to a maple
wood not far into the country. The trees were tapped, plastic tubing
runnelling the sap downhill to a sugar shack. We strolled, she ahead,
leaving talk to the winter birds, mostly chickadees. That was one
of the things I liked, that we were quiet. Possibly I was learning to live
inside fewer words.

As I watched, a dozen or so chickadees surrounded her. They think you
are a bird feeder, I said. She turned, raised her hands, palms up. One by
one the birds descended to her fingertips, then flew off. I lifted my hands.
A bird landed lightly. I closed my eyes. Only the touch of claw and air
shifting on my skin shaped the moment. The weight of a soul, I said,
then laughed at my own pretension. The bird rose in short arcs to
an overhanging beech, was replaced by another, then another.

That I later learned chickadees can be tamed is irrelevant.

Palazzo dei Medici
April 8, 1492

Lorenzo is the needle of the balance,
dying at forty-four, wasted, decrepit,
from a potion of crushed diamonds.
He lies in the great bed of inlaid
wood under an emerald canopy, his head
on velvet cushions, his crests and helmets and
pagan paintings glint in the promise of storm-
gathered light, war in Lombardy, plague and
famine, families walking south, their pots and
pans tied to donkeys.

Lorenzo summons the wild Dominican friar
to his bedside for absolution, frees the spirits
in his signet ring, a hurricane blows in and the
Medici escutcheon crumbles. Lightning strikes
the dome of Santa Maria del Fiore, Lorenzo enters
the great sea. Leonardo
remains in Milan filling his notebooks:

As from the said pool of blood proceed the veins
which spread their branches through the human
body, in just the same manner the ocean fills the
body of the earth with an infinite number of
veins of water.

Giovanni Cabotto overland to the French coast,
then to Bristol where he will sail under the
patronage of Henry VII to a rocky shore, lose the
navigational instrument in the place to be known
as New Found Land.

Always

Leave the floor till last. Soak the element drip pans, scrub the stovetop,
pry the dirt from under the lip of the sink with a paring knife. Wash
the row of vases over the cupboards, clear dead things out
of the fridge, empty mouldy yogurt, rinse the vegetable drawers. It's
always the same routine, thank goodness. Vinegar and water on chrome,
toaster oven, blender, mixer, tosser, sorter, chewer, swallower, the tap
of boiling water so you don't need a kettle. All of this restaurant-style
for two Bay Street bankers who work fourteen hour days and never darken
the door. They're expecting a baby. I suppose they plan to set the timer
and plug it in.

These houses of mine are big. When they go up for sale, they are boxed
in the real estate ads, but this seldom occurs. Mostly people stay in them
a lifetime. My houses need lawn care once a week, a sprinkling system
in the gardens so watering takes place tastefully at dawn. Twice a year
my lawns sprout tiny flags: *poison*.

My houses are being re-roofed, usually with cedar shakes. They are
bearing additions: conservatories, indoor pools, enlarged attached garages
with guest quarters on top, walled herb gardens with covered passageways
to the kitchen door. They are expanding to their lot lines. Dumpsters
squat on front walks, while within, entertainment rooms and master
suites and childrens' wings root around, looking for people.

My houses need me. They are lonely.

Corte Vecchia, Milan
March, 1493

On the eighteenth day of March 1493 Giulio
the German came to live with me.

The painted Lady with an Ermine
her gaze forever to the left
waits for her lover's return —

Magnificent Cecelia, my beloved goddess...

Who does the Master love?
He does not say.
Hidden within his workrooms:
palmate wings
cane skeleton
leather tendons
membrane of starched taffeta
muscular springs
according to specifications,
the flying machine
uccello:

The bird is an instrument
working according to mathematical
law, which instrument it is within
the capacity of man to reproduce
with all its movements, though not
with a corresponding strength,
though it is deficient only
in the power of maintaining
equilibrium.

Wings

The bankers are working on a takeover deal in Rome. They plan to travel elsewhere in Italy, final trip before the baby. I'm setting up the nursery, for extra pay. I've papered the walls with birds. Something in primary colours is what they want, so the birds are red and yellow in green trees, to stimulate the baby as early as possible. Maybe they will call it Cerebral Cortex, one of those no-sex names popular these days, Hart or Chance. I heard of a family who let the children pick names for the babies as they came along. Remote, named by Drum.

On the weekend I gathered acorns and cones in the ravine to make a mobile. The baby will learn what air is, just lying in her crib watching.

I thought I'd finished with reactions and expectations. What I wanted was a life of the small and the colourless. Glass. I would be the person everyone could see through. I would be unchanging. Any impression otherwise could be a trick of light or mere reflection. The problem here lies in the definition. Glass, while appearing solid, has all the properties of liquid. Glass flows.

Sala delle Asse Room of the Wooden Boards, Milan
April 20, 1498

Lombardy wreathed in mist.
The master labours in the dark-
ceilinged room, a forest in the vaulting,
tree limbs beribboned,
arching branches knotted over weirs and sluices,
emblems absorbed in the arboreal universe,
lateral meaning. In another smaller room,
saletta negra, small black room,
he paints grief for Il Moro:
Beatrice E'ste dead of stillborn child.

The City of the Red Lily
has burned its vanities,
books and mirrors, Sandro Botticelli's
drawings licked into flame —

Say on, Sandro! How does it strike you?
I tell you what is true,
and I have not made a success of it.

Savonarola hears another pulse
in his whitewashed cell:
the monk to hang on a gibbet
too closely resembling a cross.

Lower the crosspiece.
Let fire sever the cords
and heat lift one arm:
a Tuscany benediction
(the trace scent of olives).

Furthest

The Scholar calls me Bookworm. I'm reading certain of his books
because I'm interested in the unreliability of maps.

Seven hundred years ago two brothers sailed out of Venetian marshlands
to the Adriatic, headed north. They planned to map a snow world they
had heard described, but could not imagine. Every evening they went
ashore for food, deducing from stories the shape of the coastline ahead.
A bay given in unknown words, pictured into the dirt with a stick.
A broken oatcake to indicate an estuary. The flagon emptied is a great
river pouring itself into the sea. Dumplings floating in weak soup: islands.

No one knows if the brothers suffered scurvy, if one came to loathe
the other's laugh. Did they trade cristallo goblets for reindeer cloaks?
When is a mapmaker lost? None of these questions matter in mapping.
Only Vikna, Nordvik, Harstad.

Erroneous cartography is another matter. The brothers painted a tiny ship
on the sea near Greenland, when they made their map. Greenland they
drew as a long thin curve attached to Norway, wrapped around Iceland.
Seven islands float at the westerly edge of the sea. The Venetians set
arctic exploration back two centuries.

Fortunately for maps, we keep losing the way.

Corte Vecchia, Milan
October 24, 1499

Leonardo paints.

He trembles. He adjusts the glow
from the circular window, working
pulleys which raise the painting
in the southeast corner of the palace.
Today he brushes in the icy mountains
behind her, playing blue tones against
the green silk of her gown
Isabella of Aragon
husband murdered
son captive
Spain a memory in red
her smile unvanquished.
He must work quickly
for soon the King of France
will sustain a grazing blow
to the head while hurrying
to a tennis match and be dead
within the day.
His successor will rush to invade
Italy for revenge and although
the citadel is supplied for a three-
month siege and is defended
by three thousand mercenaries,
the Duchy will be surrendered
on a bribe. Leonardo will flee
to the city of canals, in a sack
the portrait not yet known as
Mona Lisa.

Gravity

As I walked past Blessed Sacrament Church on the way home from work, a lone male cardinal sent his two-part whistle out over the park. He sang as though he loved me. Spring, I thought.

I live on Rogers Road in a small house beside the jeweller. In the evenings, after a light supper and milky tea, I listen to the news at eleven. I have trouble falling asleep, so often I listen to AM radio, talk shows, on into the night. The sheer craziness of the conversation soothes. When I do sleep deeply, I dream. In my dreams I am flying, with spiritual purpose it seems, above a white landscape.

In my dreams there is no social intercourse, sanity is entirely personal. Cells divide with regular rhythm. I don't know how I know this, but I do.

I recognize the long crease in my hand for what it is, and I am flying above the treeline.

For nine years I've been within loss, scraping at its sides like a dog. I suppose I am trying to make a den, even set out plants. The child remembered indistinctly, a poor rubbing from brass.

Today the subway stalled between Davisville and St Clair, affording a clear view of the cemetery. My grade five teacher used to take us to the graveyard for the trees. Over a hundred kinds, she said. My parents are buried there. The only stone I visit says *Lost*. Nothing more.

Venice
March 13, 1500

In a small room above the shop of Lorenzo
Gignasco, instrument-maker, Leonardo
makes notes: *The eye which is called the window
of the soul. And if the poet serves
the understanding by way of the ear,
the painter does so by the eye.*

Or by freedom. From the height of the Campanile
Leonardo observes Scander Bassa the Turk
burn his way back to Bosnia.
Perfidious smoke and torched farmsteads,
cavalry formations scattering,

the particulars of the view forfeit,
leached of colour and observable detail
just as the great fresco in the refectory
at Santa Marie della Grazie day
by day gave itself up to damp,

The Last Supper: the bread half cut through
by the knife, overturned glass, slender fingers,
blue embroidered stripes in the tablecloth,
the betrayal blurred to shadowed ruin,
the intention of the soul, if you like.

*If liberty is dear to you, do not reveal that my
face is the prison house of love.*

Air

There will be no consolation, says the Scholar. Without the smallest consolation, I say, it is possible to go haywire.

Once love reigned over my life like a mad sovereign. Love will drive a person to prison and exile, both. To pack up everything and go, without thought, without choice. I walked in, locked all the doors behind me, relinquished the keys. I was the lady and the lady-in-waiting, dressing and undressing in airless rooms, scarlet banners hung over the windows to keep in perfume and meandering music. Disgrace meant nothing. My family lost to me.

But even mad love will fail for lack of air and regular routine. Mad love will wander off, back to the pebbles and stones of the known way. We live in loneliness that should kill us, but doesn't. What will keep us going is simpler, more elemental. Say, water.

The neighbourhood I go home to is one up from poor. The houses are small, war-time. People work on them, yelling back and forth as they paint the front doors lime green and add porches. The tiny backyards are fenced. Most have gardens. Mine is blue. Lilac, iris, delphinium. Love-in-a-Mist which I grow for the name. Late summer its petals fall. The leaves toughen, rise and curl around the green fruit like thorns. Five spires. Sometimes birds land on the tips, not bothered by their sharpness. Its other name is Devil-in-a-Bush.

I say that I practise meditation in the garden. Emptying my mind. What happens in the garden more closely resembles sorting. What can be remembered.

Porto Cesenatico
September 6, 1502

The painter is weary of his brushes
non può patire il pennello,
short of cash: presto!
architect and general engineer
becomes Inspector of Fortifications
for Cesare Borgia
who would kill as soon as offer his
elegant smile.

Leonardo is a caravan festooned
with lenses and parabolic mirrors
making leisurely progress from strong point
to military outpost, reverse script filling
notebooks with engines of war,
inventions for the patron who has little use
for maps or floral investigation, but we
who follow have been marvellously served:

the eccentricity of tree trunks,
the accretion of annual growth.

For the painter there will be no escape,
only the last angel,
a final weightless passage
lit by sixty tapers
borne by sixty paupers.

Descend

The note I left on the kitchen table for Mrs. Nakamura niggles. It was just meant to be light and cheer her up, a bit of a joke between us about the parties Mr. Nakamura throws for his business friends. I'm a note-leaver. I used to think people could be surprised out of unhappiness by having their sadness noticed. Now I think I leave the notes because I've always made a poultice of myself to be applied to others.

I've been afraid as long I can remember. Once I realized I'd been waiting to fall in love all my life — my hollowed-out childhood more or less leading me down the garden path to the serpent and the apple in one fell swoop — I didn't just fall, I rushed to the precipice and hurled myself over into love, which failed me. Later I failed love, the marriage, the kids.

I wonder now about fear. When I was young dying scared me, until I saw it, right under my nose.

If all the things I am afraid of were that simple, I could have done everything.

Piazza del Signoria, Florence
February 11, 1504

I have wasted my hours.

The Committee: Perugino, Botticelli, Lippi,
Le Cronaca, Andrea della Robbia, Leonardo da Vinci.

The Decision: site for a colossal white-limbed David
whose mass and volume will refigure carving.

The Debate: place the statue within the Loggia
dei Lanzi to afford it protection from weather,
or accede to its maker who would have his way as
would half the city, in stone opinions hurled.

The Winner: in dogskin boots, marble-dusted
Michelangelo Buonarroti, broken-nosed, fearless,
who would have his sculpted hero where he would
have him, the devil take the hindmost.

Leonardo's Failures to date: squaring the circle
(Archimedes), unfinished work (The Last Supper,
The Great Horse, The Virgin and The Child with
Saint Anne), flying.

*The great bird will take its first flight from the back
of the Great Swan, dumbfounding the universe,
overwhelming with its renown all writings, and
bring eternal glory to its birthplace.*

Condensed

The Scholar walked into his life today. He's in love. Seems he doesn't care that his father, the cabinet minister, disapproves. More than disapproves. Refuses him entry, threatens to disinherit. No word from the mother. It's that kind of family. I had one, too. The Scholar doesn't care. His lover has moved in. An actor, beautiful, blond curls, irresistible. All day they talk to me, together and apart. I get very little done. Neither does the Scholar. The Actor enters a room. It becomes an unmade bed. Nobody minds.

The bankers are back. They loved Tuscany and brought me a book about painters. They try to draw me out, improve my outlook.

Right away they threw themselves a gathering, called it Advent. Used to be called a baby shower. They asked me to help with the food, trays of hot and cold, antipasto mostly. Classical. The guests were downtowners. Associates, they called themselves. Used to be called friends. All from firms with five names, three anglo, two ethnic. They talked business, the women especially. Markets. Commodities.

Make a list of instructions for this baby, I promise myself. Leave it somewhere prominent. Don't get involved. Pain stirs, a houseful of assassins waking up.

The bankers have taken to calling me Firenze, to remind themselves of Italy.

Hall of the Great Council, Florence
April 2, 1505

He comes down from the ochre hills, small notebook
in his cloak: *The bird I have described ought
to be able by the help of wind to rise to a great height, and
this will prove to be its safety...*

Leonardo will paint what he has to say about war
(*pazzia bestialissima*) the Battle of Anghiari,
a frenzy of horses arrows river and dust.

Zoroastre de Peretola prepares and smoothes:
Venetian sponges and Alexandrian white, affixing
smoke on smoke to the plaster wall, linseed oil,
Greek pitch.

In the shadows hides a youth from Urbino, Raphael.
He is twenty. He watches Leonardo mix colour, a
recipe taken from Pliny the Elder, stoke the coal fire

which is too far from the painted wall
and the colours begin to run. The painting weeps
itself into the floor leaving only its outline,
handwriting on the wall.

Movement

Mrs. Mullock died last week. Unexpectedly. I believe she gave up. Alone in that big house, her kids never looking in. All that business about the son and the abuse didn't wash with me. Mrs. Mullock may have been batty but she wasn't wicked. Her son wrote the story into a play and broke her heart. She spent the last month in bed. She'd eat toast and soup when I made them. I never knew what happened when I wasn't there. At the end she was skin and bones. Call the doctor, I told her. She nodded.

The silver, vases of late lobelia, sandwiches, the circular ones, and they all showed up: the daughters, the friends Mrs. Mullock phoned once in a while, the bankers, even the son. They ate and drank after the cemetery, poked around in the cupboards and drawers, everyone curious. Mrs. Nakamura kept her eye on things. My flowers got put aside for the floral arrangements — too blue someone said. The Scholar spoke. He talked about the solitary life, the need to celebrate contemplation. People nodded. Frankly I retreated to the kitchen with the Actor.

I believe Mrs. Mullock chose to die and I am angry with her. Being lonely is no excuse. It's one thing to die. Another to want to. What about the people who live on after, what story do they believe?

Leonardo's Studio, Milan
Winter, 1510

I look to finish all this anatomy.

In service to the King of France
he dissected ten bodies with care,
removing particles of flesh from veins
to render his knowledge complete;
with great diligence the red chalk
drawings of nerves and muscles
fall to the floor at his feet, surpassing
beauty;

he eats baked onion with a milled ryecake,
the piece of chalk lying on the stool
to his side will go on to describe
a cloud in the shape of an immense mountain
full of red rocks which lies above
a wide expanse leading to hills
where the Alps encounter the Lombardy
plain, sealife vestiges enclosed within:
leviathan, skeletons of ships.

Sufficient for us is the testimony
of things produced in the salt waters
and now found again in the high mountains
far from the seas.

Pivot

Turned into the drugstore for calcium and shampoo and he, behind, didn't
see me. I caught him out of the corner of my eye. Last I'd heard from
the kids he was living out by the airport. He'd given up on me, they said.

Down the cosmetic aisle, I made for the blood pressure test. Put my arm
in the cuff, pumped it full to make me stay put. Didn't dare look at
the reading, released the pressure when my hand went numb, just long
enough for him to pay and leave.

Drugstores and hardware outlets, I find them calming. Easing myself out
of the booth, I went looking for earplugs. I don't sleep, haven't since.
Before I go to bed I take evening primrose with herbal tea. Sometimes
I dump in a shot of sherry. Then for sure I have the flying dreams. Even
though I'm afraid of heights. Stepladders, cliffs.

In the pen and pencil section, I grabbed a pen with the finest nib and
wrote all the arctic names I could remember — Ellesmere, Beaufort,
Amundsen, Barrow, Lancaster, Baffin, Boothia, Davis, Victoria, Hudson,
Desolation — because I knew once and for all that I would never go.

The Belvedere, Rome
December 11, 1514

A man who is in despair you should draw turning his
knife against himself, and rending his garments with
his hands, and one of his hands should be in the act of
tearing open his wound.

On the back of a letter from his family
in Florence he makes several geometric patterns
while considering the lapse of his sister-in-law
into madness. These unhappy years, pushed aside.
Finished, the Master and sister both.

For he must descend into the Great Deluge,
imagine once and for all the catechism
of anguish: teeming wildness, lamentation
of uprooted cypress, casual plains
covered in bedsteads and snakes, all manner
of mammals huddled together
under unspeakable wind,
unleashed flooding carnage.

Oh how the mothers brandish their fists
against the heavens and weep
for the drowned sons they hold on their knees,
howling curses on the wrath of the gods.

And, oh, the drawing in black lead and ink wash
absorbed in the leaves of the notebook.

Impetus

This afternoon shifted in the space of six words. I quit work late today,
everybody, everywhere. A reversal. Turns out Mrs. Mullock left me
money. *Silver stock, software shares*, the lawyer said, *a few*. Irony, I
told the mirrored doors in the elevator, descending forty-six floors. Its
glass gave me back, exactly reversed, without streaks. The doors opened
to the foyer, marble walls with weather trapped in the layers like a
glacier. I studied the wall for a sign.

Contrary to my rules, I bought a new jacket. Red, deep claret. Not black
or beige. Bold. Forthright. Expansive. My words spread out as the day
progressed. Possibly I'll have bath oil, I said, sandalwood, I said, as
I wandered through the store and out to the street, smelling the scent
rising out of the carrier bag on my way home through strewn leaves up
the hill, out of the ravine.

Have I spent long enough in the partial, letting it stand for the whole, all
that will outlive me? The almanac predicts a hard winter. Even
in the worst weather, the ice pack moves.

I'm thinking presently of slow travel down the St Lawrence for the white
whales in the Saguenay. Maybe Antigonish, then icebergs in Conception
Bay. What keeps me here?

Sometimes now or never arrives edgewise, within reach, pronounceable
as the last words spoken by the last friend.

Florence
late autumn, 1516

Beyond the city gates
he ate his traveller's meal:
roast chestnuts and Orvieto wine, opened the cage
to release the warblers and hunting hawk,
finally the young swan who will ascend
Mont Tabora, observe the radiant glacier,
and descend with Leonardo into France.

The Manor Cloux —
The domain: three acres of gardens,
a meadow, a vineyard, fishing stream with doves.
The building: a chapel, large studio, bedrooms.
The terms: an annual pension of a thousand *ecus soleil*.

Paralysis will seize his right arm; he will draw
little, paint less; instead pass the days
in conversation with the young king,
amaze him with tales of lizards dipped in silver,
the perfection of octagons.

In youth acquire that which may requite you
for the deprivations of old age; and if you are
mindful that old age has wisdom for its food,
you will so exert yourself in youth, that your
old age will not lack sustenance.

Instrument

In the way a pane of glass is finished by bevelled edges, it could end this way: she goes.

Down the St Lawrence to the sea, over Cabot Strait by dead reckoning. The shore, highly inclined slate. To the south, the continuous presence of icebergs, and the sea's fluid attentions to the shore.
The tenderness of washing.

At a rock-hardened cove called Frogmarsh, near Brigus, the woman walks toward a wharf on soft capelin spawn. She gives off uncertainty as ice emits cold, a forecast of itself. She stoops to pick up the encrusted shape rocking in the briny shallows, its differential gears locked solid.

More closely: the weight of iron in her hand, despite degrees of correction lost to corrosion, yields her position: here, found at last.

It would not be so neat. Over and over the sea washes its hands of such answers.

Amboise, France
May 2, 1519

Observe the light and consider its beauty.
Blink your eye and look at it.

Stooped figure ascends the spiral
staircase. He is bearded, this old
man who has been devoted to curves
of cascading hair and water, ascending
step by step past dark corridors
beyond rooms teeming with articles of
invention, tracing the form of a shell
found on the Italian north-west coast
and nowhere else, *Voluta vespertilio,*
his soft leather boots tracking
sinistral arc acceding into arc:
a mind opening or the lines of
movement made by birds as
they rise.

Constancy. Not he who begins
but he who endures.

High above the Loire
the faithful Melzi weeps.
Seized by sudden illness,
the King's Painter dies
in the arms of France.

Flying

The geese return. I watch the plainness of their travel, no arabesques, no
larking about. Days go by without a conversation. There is plenty
to watch, which is different from trying not to think. When the weather
turns, we go indoors. I am reading *Sailing Directions for the Island
of Newfoundland and the Adjacent Coast of Labrador, 1862*, aloud.
This may be as close as I get. Navigation was difficult then as now, I tell
the baby. Taking soundings, for instance, has always been unreliable.

The past is a spoon I lift to my cheek for coolness. My life may be
threadbare but it's serviceable. The bankers return from Hong Kong
tomorrow. The baby smiled while they were gone.

It came to me yesterday that you have been with me all along, here,
haphazard in the groundcover ferns, curled like questions. In the
questions themselves. Now that I know we will never be joined or parted,
I will go ahead into all that is left for me.

Note

It is impossible to estimate the original number of Leonardo's manuscripts. The Secretary of the Cardinal of Aragon, who visited him at Cloux, reported that he saw "an infinite number of volumes all in the vulgar tongue." Many were in reverse writing.

By the terms of his will, all texts were bequeathed to Francesco Melzi, a pupil and companion, who returned with them to Milan. By the time the famous biographer of Renaissance artists, Vasari, saw the manuscripts, he noted that Melzi guarded his inheritance as though the notebooks were holy relics. Apparently his heirs did not, and were responsible for their gradual dispersal.

The largest of the manuscripts, Codice Atlantico, resides in the Library of the Institut de France.

Forster I, II, III, the Forster Bequest MSS. I, II, III, is found in the Victoria and Albert Museum, London.

Codex Leicester, formerly in the collection of the Earl of Leicester, belongs to Bill Gates, Microsoft.

Quaderni d'Anatomica I-IV, is in the Royal Collection, Royal Library, Windsor.

Codex on the Flight of Birds, Sul Volo degil Uccelli, is in the Royal Library, Turin.

Acknowledgements

This book is for my friends, who believed in it.

My thanks to the editors of the publications in which some of these poems previously appeared: *Close to the Heart* (English Garden Publishers) 1996, *At the Threshold: Writing Towards the Year 2000* (Porcepic Books, Beach Holme Publishing) 1999, Pottersfield Portfolio.

This book has been long in the making. For a while I wasn't sure what I was building, but I knew I had a lot of helpers. I owe thanks to Steve Page who nabbed a 10-pound compendium on Leonardo da Vinci 20 years ago at our rural library book sale, and started the whole thing. Hometown crowd: Donna Vittorio, Steven Heighton, Barbara Schlafer, Elizabeth Greene, Carolyn Smart, Margaret Hooey and Helen Humphreys. Further afield: Kathy Fretwell and Jan Zwicky read early drafts, as did Don McKay who loaned me a phrase for a poem title, Sue Goyette, Maureen Hynes and Anne Corkett provided years of steadiness; I am grateful for the many benefits of my two residencies at the Banff Centre's Writing Studio amid a generous writing community whose work I respect and friendship I treasure.

Beth Follett's sound judgement, her attentiveness and acumen, has meant that the readying of the book for publication rolled out in painless pleasure.

Joan Geramita's contribution to this book has been essential, her letters and conversations and thoughts pivotal. Hers are the words of The Mathematician, disturbing and compelling, that required of me the best answer I could give.

Finally, and most especially, I owe a great debt to my editor, Erin Mouré, who pushed me and my enterprise into bigger water some years ago, and then stuck around to function as breeze, rudder, mechanic and, occasionally, tug, to ensure that the words and I weathered the voyage.

Joanne Page lives in Kingston, Ontario. She is a visual artist and the author of *The River & The Lake* (Quarry Press, 1993), and the editor of *Arguments with the World: The Essays of Bronwen Wallace* (Quarry Press, 1992). For many years, she was an editorial page columnist for the Kingston Whig-Standard and an editor for Quarry Magazine.

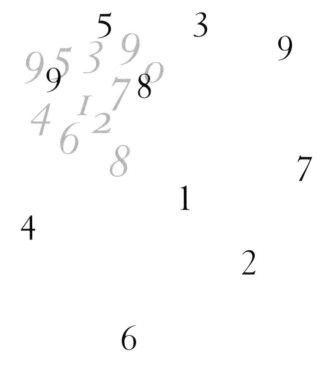